ABRAHAM LINCOLN

Mystic Chords of Memory

ABRAHAM LINCOLN

Mystic Chords of Memory

A SELECTION FROM
LINCOLN'S WRITINGS

Edited by Larry Shapiro

Book-of-the-Month Club · New York

FRONTISPIECE
*Abraham Lincoln from a photograph made by Anthony Berger
at Mathew Brady's gallery, Washington, D.C., February 9, 1864.
Detail. Library of Congress*

*All quotations from Lincoln in this book have been reprinted
from* The Collected Works of Abraham Lincoln, *edited by Roy
P. Basler. Copyright, 1953, by the Abraham Lincoln
Association. Reprinted by permission of
Rutgers University Press.*

In matters of spelling and grammar this book follows
The Collected Works *in reproducing Lincoln's own usage.*

*All introductory material
copyright © 1984 by Book-of-the-Month Club, Inc.*
All rights reserved.

is a registered trademark of Book-of-the-Month Club, Inc.

Manufactured in the United States of America

CONTENTS

"The mystic chords of memory, stretching from every battle-field, and patriot grave, to every living heart and hearthstone, all over this broad land, will yet swell the chorus of the Union, when again touched, as surely they will be, by the better angels of our nature."

—From the First Inaugural Address, March 4, 1861

☆ I ☆
"Always a Whig in Politics"
The Early Years

AUTOBIOGRAPHICAL SKETCH, 1859

By the winter of 1859, Abraham Lincoln was working quietly to win the Republican Party's presidential nomination—propriety forbade a candidate to run openly for the nomination. He supplied this account of his early years to a Pennsylvania backer, who in turn passed it on to a political journalist. Expanded into a newspaper biography, the piece was much reprinted in Republican papers and helped Lincoln get the nomination at the Republican Convention the following June.

J. W. Fell, Esq   Springfield,
My dear Sir: Dec. 20. 1859

Herewith is a little sketch, as you requested. There is not much of it, for the reason, I suppose, that there is not much of me.

If any thing be made out of it, I wish it to be modest, and not to go beyond the material. If it were thought necessary to incorporate any thing from any of my speeches, I suppose there would be no objection. Of course it must not appear to have been written by myself. Yours very truly   A. LINCOLN

I was born Feb. 12, 1809, in Hardin County, Kentucky. My parents were both born in Virginia, of undistinguished families —second families, perhaps I should say. My mother, who died in my tenth year, was of a family of the name of Hanks, some of whom now reside in Adams, and others in Macon counties, Illinois. My paternal grandfather, Abraham Lincoln, emigrated from Rockingham County, Virginia, to Kentucky, about 1781 or 2, where, a year or two later, he was killed by indians, not in battle, but by stealth, when [where?] he was laboring to open a farm in the forest. His ancestors, who were quakers, went to

Virginia from Berks County, Pennsylvania. An effort to identify them with the New-England family of the same name ended in nothing more definite, than a similarity of Christian names in both families, such as Enoch, Levi, Mordecai, Solomon, Abraham, and the like.

My father, at the death of his father, was but six years of age; and he grew up, litterally without education. He removed from Kentucky to what is now Spencer county, Indiana, in my eighth year. We reached our new home about the time the State came into the Union. It was a wild region, with many bears and other wild animals still in the woods. There I grew up. There were some schools, so called; but no qualification was ever required of a teacher, beyond *"readin, writin, and cipherin,"* to the Rule of Three. If a straggler supposed to understand latin, happened to sojourn in the neighborhood, he was looked upon as a wizzard. There was absolutely nothing to excite ambition for education. Of course when I came of age I did not know much. Still somehow, I could read, write, and cipher to the Rule of Three; but that was all. I have not been to school since. The little advance I now have upon this store of education, I have picked up from time to time under the pressure of necessity.

I was raised to farm work, which I continued till I was twenty two. At twenty one I came to Illinois, and passed the first year in Illinois—Macon county. Then I got to New-Salem, (at that time in Sangamon, now in Menard county, where I remained a year as a sort of Clerk in a store. Then came the Black-Hawk war; and I was elected a Captain of Volunteers—a success which gave me more pleasure than any I have had since. I went the campaign, was elated, ran for the Legislature the same year (1832) and was beaten—the only time I have been beaten by the people. The next, and three succeeding biennial elections, I was elected to the Legislature. I was not a candidate afterwards. During this Legislative period I had studied law, and removed to

Springfield to practice it. In 1846 I was once elected to the lower House of Congress. Was not a candidate for re-election. From 1849 to 1854, both inclusive, practiced law more assiduously than ever before. Always a whig in politics, and generally on the whig electoral tickets, making active canvasses. I was losing interest in politics, when the repeal of the Missouri Compromise aroused me again. What I have done since then is pretty well known.

If any personal description of me is thought desirable, it may be said, I am, in height, six feet, four inches, nearly; lean in flesh, weighing, on an average, one hundred and eighty pounds; dark complexion, with coarse black hair, and grèy eyes—no other marks or brands recollected. Yours very truly   A. LINCOLN

Hon. J. W. Fell.

☆

FROM A CAMPAIGN
ANNOUNCEMENT, 1832

This is Lincoln's voice at the outset of his political career: a 23-year-old, with experience as a ferryman, storekeeper, farm hand and railsplitter, announcing his candidacy for the Illinois State Legislature. Lincoln had help on the piece from a local schoolteacher, and much of it sounds like what any conventionally pious young man might have written. But we can also recognize the authentic Lincoln in the earnestness of the piece, the expressions of humility, the innate conservatism.

Upon the subject of education, not presuming to dictate any plan or system respecting it, I can only say that I view it as the most important subject which we as a people can be engaged in. . . . For my part, I desire to see the time when education, and by its means, morality, sobriety, enterprise and industry, shall become much more general than at present, and should be gratified to have it in my power to contribute something to the advancement of any measure which might have a tendency to accelerate the happy period.

With regard to existing laws, some alterations are thought to be necessary. . . . But considering the great probability that the framers of those laws were wiser than myself, I should prefer [not?] meddling with them, unless they were first attacked by others, in which case I should feel it both a privilege and a duty to take that stand, which in my view, might tend most to the advancement of justice.

But, Fellow-Citizens, I shall conclude. Considering the great degree of modesty which should always attend youth, it is probable I have already been more presuming than becomes me. However, upon the subjects of which I have treated, I have spoken as I thought. I may be wrong in regard to any or all of them; but holding it a sound maxim, that it is better to be only sometimes right, than at all times wrong, so soon as I discover my opinions to be erroneous, I shall be ready to renounce them.

Every man is said to have his peculiar ambition. Whether it be true or not, I can say for one that I have no other so great as that of being truly esteemed of my fellow men, by rendering myself worthy of their esteem. How far I shall succeed in gratifying this ambition, is yet to be developed. I am young and unknown to many of you. I was born and have ever remained in the most humble walks of life. I have no wealthy or popular relations to recommend me. My case is thrown exclusively upon the independent voters of this county, and if elected they will have conferred a favor upon me, for which I shall be unremitting in my labors to compensate. But if the good people in their wisdom shall see fit to keep me in the background, I have been too familiar with disappointments to be very much chagrined. Your friend and fellow-citizen,   A. LINCOLN
New Salem, March 9, 1832.

CAMPAIGN ANNOUNCEMENT, 1836

In the 1832 contest Lincoln finished eighth in a field of thirteen, but in 1836 he tried again and was elected. This campaign announcement, which appeared in the Sangamo Journal, *sounds folksy compared with the 1832 document, but the candidate's platform is again conservative in its Whig Party emphasis on cautious improvements to benefit commerce. Illinois voting law of the time was actually more liberal than Lincoln's position, since it gave the vote to all adult white males.*

NEW SALEM, June 13, 1836.

To the Editor of the Journal:

In your paper of last Saturday, I see a communication over the signature of "Many Voters," in which the candidates who are announced in the Journal, are called upon to "show their hands." Agreed. Here's mine!

I go for all sharing the privileges of the government, who assist in bearing its burthens. Consequently I go for admitting all whites to the right of suffrage, who pay taxes or bear arms, (by no means excluding females.)

If elected, I shall consider the whole people of Sangamon my constituents, as well those that oppose, as those that support me.

While acting as their representative, I shall be governed by their will, on all subjects upon which I have the means of knowing what their will is; and upon all others, I shall do what my own judgment teaches me will best advance their interests. Whether elected or not, I go for distributing the proceeds of the sales of the public lands to the several states, to enable our state, in common with others, to dig canals and construct rail roads, without borrowing money and paying interest on it.

If alive on the first Monday in November, I shall vote for Hugh L. White for President. Very respectfully,   A. LINCOLN.

☆

EXCERPT FROM LINCOLN'S SPEECH
TO THE YOUNG MEN'S LYCEUM
OF SPRINGFIELD, 1838

In January 1838, the young legislator was invited to address the Springfield cultural organization on a topic of his choice. Lincoln spoke on "the perpetuation of our political institutions," and warned that the rise of mob violence suggested a breakdown in the rule of law that might be irreversible. And he expressed a concern that would haunt him and shape his political personality: what would become of America when its founding fathers were gone, their disciples were gone, and the new generation had no great leaders to inspire it with the original ideals of the republic?

I do not mean to say, that the scenes of the revolution *are now* or *ever will be* entirely forgotten; but that like every thing else, they must fade upon the memory of the world, and grow more and more dim by the lapse of time. In history, we hope, they will be read of, and recounted, so long as the bible shall be read;— but even granting that they will, their influence *cannot be* what it heretofore has been. Even then, they *cannot be* so universally known, nor so vividly felt, as they were by the generation just gone to rest. At the close of that struggle, nearly every adult male had been a participator in some of its scenes. The consequence was, that of those scenes, in the form of a husband, a father, a son or a brother, a *living history was* to be found in every family—a history bearing the indubitable testimonies of its own authenticity, in the limbs mangled, in the scars of wounds received, in the midst of the very scenes related—a history, too, that could be read and understood alike by all, the wise and the ignorant, the learned and the unlearned. But *those* histories are gone. They *can* be read no more forever. They *were* a fortress of strength; but, what invading foemen could *never do*, the silent artillery of time *has done;* the levelling of its walls. They are gone. They *were* a forest of giant oaks; but the all-resistless hurricane has swept over them, and left only, here and there, a lonely trunk, despoiled of its verdure, shorn of its foliage; unshading and unshaded, to murmur in a few more gentle breezes, and to combat with its mutilated limbs, a few more ruder storms, then to sink, and be no more.

They *were* the pillars of the temple of liberty; and now, that they have crumbled away, that temple must fall, unless we, their descendants, supply their places with other pillars, hewn from the solid quarry of sober reason. Passion has helped us; but can do so no more. It will in future be our enemy. Reason, cold, calculating, unimpassioned reason must furnish all the materials for our future support and defence.

☆

FROM LETTERS TO
MARY TODD LINCOLN, 1848

Lincoln's law partner, William Herndon, is the principal source for stories about how Lincoln suffered in his marriage. But the bad feeling between Herndon and Mrs. Lincoln distorted his perceptions. These letters suggest that Lincoln's marriage, like most, was too complex to be called good or bad. Lincoln himself wrote almost nothing about the marriage, apart from a comment in a letter after the first week: "Nothing new here, except my marrying, which to me, is a matter of profound wonder."

Washington, April 16– 1848–

Dear Mary:

In this troublesome world, we are never quite satisfied. When you were here, I thought you hindered me some in attending to business; but now, having nothing but business—no variety—it has grown exceedingly tasteless to me. I hate to sit down and direct documents, and I hate to stay in this old room by myself.

You know I told you in last sunday's letter, I was going to make a little speech during the week; but the week has passed away without my getting a chance to do so; and now my interest in the subject has passed away too. Your second and third letters have been received since I wrote before. Dear Eddy thinks father is "*gone tapila*[.]" Has any further discovery been made as to the breaking into your grand-mother's house? If I were she, I would not remain there alone. You mention that your uncle John Parker is likely to be at Lexington. Dont forget to present him my very kindest regards.

I went yesterday to hunt the little plaid stockings, as you wished; but found that McKnight has quit business, and Allen had not a single pair of the description you give, and only one plaid pair of any sort that I thought would fit "Eddy's dear little feet." I have a notion to make another trial to-morrow morning. If I could get them, I have an excellent chance of sending them. Mr. Warrick Tunstall, of St. Louis is here. He is to leave early this week, and to go by Lexington. He says he knows you, and will call to see you; and he voluntarily asked, if I had not some package to send to you.

I wish you to enjoy yourself in every possible way; but is there no danger of wounding the feelings of your good father, by being so openly intimate with the Wickliffe family?

Mrs. Broome has not removed yet; but she thinks of doing so to-morrow. All the house—or rather, all with whom you were on decided good terms—send their love to you. The others say nothing.

Very soon after you went away, I got what I think a very pretty set of shirt-bosom studs—modest little ones, jet, set in gold, only costing 50 cents a piece, or 1.50 for the whole.

Suppose you do not prefix the "Hon" to the address on your letters to me any more. I like the letters very much, but I would rather they should not have that upon them. It is not necessary, as I suppose you have thought, to have them to come free.

And you are entirely free from head-ache? That is good—good—considering it is the first spring you have been free from it since we were acquainted. I am afraid you will get so well, and fat, and young, as to be wanting to marry again. Tell Louisa I want her to watch you a little for me. Get weighed, and write me how much you weigh.

I did not get rid of the impression of that foolish dream about dear Bobby till I got your letter written the same day. What did he and Eddy think of the little letters father sent them? Dont let the blessed fellows forget father.

A day or two ago Mr. Strong, here in Congress, said to me that Matilda would visit here within two or three weeks. Suppose you write her a letter, and enclose it in one of mine; and if she comes I will deliver it to her, and if she does not, I will send it to her.

Most affectionately   A. LINCOLN

Washington, June 12. 1848—

My dear wife:

On my return from Philadelphia, yesterday, where, in my anxiety I had been led to attend the whig convention I found your last letter. I was so tired and sleepy, having ridden all night, that I could not answer it till to-day; and now I have to do so in the H.R. The leading matter in your letter, is your wish to return to this side of the Mountains. Will you be a *good girl* in all things, if I consent? Then come along, and that as *soon* as possible. Having got the idea in my head, I shall be impatient till I see you. You will not have money enough to bring you; but I presume your uncle will supply you, and I will refund him here. By the way you do not mention whether you have received the fifty dollars I sent you. I do not much fear but that you got it; because the want of it would have induced you [to?] say something in relation to it. If your uncle is already at Lexington, you might induce him to start on earlier than the first of July; he could stay in Kentucky longer on his return, and so make up for lost time. Since I began this letter, the H.R. has passed a resolution for adjourning on the 17th. July, which probably will pass the Senate. I hope this letter will not be disagreeable to you; which, together with the circumstances under which I write, I hope will excuse me for not writing a longer one. Come on just as soon as you can. I want to see you, and our dear—*dear* boys very much. Every body here wants to see our dear Bobby. Affectionately

A. LINCOLN

☆

LINCOLN IN CONGRESS:
FOUR LETTERS

In about 1843, Lincoln began maneuvering to obtain the Whig nomination to run for the U.S. Congress; but the nomination didn't come until 1846. Herndon, who joined in partnership with Lincoln about this time, later wrote: "That man who thinks Lincoln calmly gathered his robes about him, waiting for the people to call him, has a very erroneous knowledge of Lincoln. He was always calculating and planning ahead. His ambition was a little engine that knew no rest."

Lincoln was a one-term congressman, and the high and low point occurred within a few weeks of the beginning of the term, when he expressed the Whig Party's opposition to the war with Mexico. His speech, which called President Polk a "bewildered, confounded, and miserably perplexed man," had a calamitous impact back in Illinois, where the war was popular. Well before he received a surprise request for an autograph, Lincoln was aware that his career was probably doomed.

To Richard S. Thomas

Springfield, Ills., Feb. 14, 1843.

Friend Richard: ... Now if you should hear any one say that Lincoln don't want to go to Congress, I wish you as a personal friend of mine, would tell him you have reason to believe he is mistaken. The truth is, I would like to go very much. Still, circumstances may happen which may prevent my being a candidate.

If there are any who be my friends in such an enterprise, what I now want is that they shall not throw me away just yet. Yours as ever,   A. LINCOLN

To William H. Herndon

Washington, January 8, 1848.

Dear William: Your letter of December 27 was received a day or two ago. I am much obliged to you for the trouble you have taken, and promise to take in my little business there. As to speechmaking, by way of getting the hang of the House I made a little speech two or three days ago on a post-office question of no general interest. I find speaking here and elsewhere about the same thing. I was about as badly scared, and no worse, as I am when I speak in court. I expect to make one within a week or two, in which I hope to succeed well enough to wish you to see it.

To William H. Herndon

February 1, 1848

I do not mean this letter for the public, but for you. Before it reaches you, you will have seen and read my pamphlet speech, and perhaps, scared anew, by it. After you get over your scare, read it over again, sentence by sentence, and tell me honestly what you think of it. I condensed all I could for fear of being cut off by the hour rule, and when I got through, I had spoke but 45 minutes. Yours forever   A. LINCOLN

To C. U. Schlater

Mr. C. U. Schlater: Washington,
Dear Sir: Jan: 5. 1849

Your note, requesting my "signature with a sentiment" was received, and should have been answered long since, but that it was mislaid. I am not a very sentimental man; and the best sentiment I can think of is, that if you collect the signatures of all persons who are no less distinguished than I, you will have a very undistinguishing mass of names. Very respectfully

A. LINCOLN

☆

☆ II ☆
"A Continual Torment"
The Slavery Controversy

FRAGMENT ON SLAVERY, 1854

Lincoln's political silence lasted until the fall of 1854, a few months after this fragment was probably written, when he came forward to speak out against the possibility that slavery might be extended beyond the South until it became a national institution. At this point in his isolation he was brooding about a custom he had disapproved of but considered politically "a minor question."

[July 1, 1854?]

If A. can prove, however conclusively, that he may, of right, enslave B.—why may not B. snatch the same argument, and prove equally, that he may enslave A?—

You say A. is white, and B. is black. It is *color*, then; the lighter, having the right to enslave the darker? Take care. By this rule, you are to be slave to the first man you meet, with a fairer skin than your own.

You do not mean *color* exactly?—You mean the whites are *intellectually* the superiors of the blacks, and, therefore have the right to enslave them? Take care again. By this rule, you are to be slave to the first man you meet, with an intellect superior to your own.

But, say you, it is a question of *interest*; and, if you can make it your *interest*, you have the right to enslave another. Very well. And if he can make it his interest, he has the right to enslave you.

☆

FROM A LETTER TO JOSHUA SPEED, 1855

During the years of Lincoln's political exile the issue of slavery had intensified the differences between North and South. The issue of sectional difference takes on an unusually personal tone in this letter to Speed, who had been Lincoln's closest friend when both men lived in Illinois but who had since returned to his native Kentucky.

Springfield, Aug: 24, 1855

Dear Speed:

You know what a poor correspondent I am. Ever since I received your very agreeable letter of the 22nd. of May I have been intending to write you in answer to it. You suggest that in political action now, you and I would differ. I suppose we would; not quite as much, however, as you may think. You know I dislike slavery; and you fully admit the abstract wrong of it. So far there is no cause of difference. But you say that sooner than yield your legal right to the slave—especially at the bidding of those who are not themselves interested, you would see the Union dissolved. I am not aware that *any one* is bidding you to yield that right; very certainly *I* am not. I leave that matter entirely to yourself. I also acknowledge *your* rights and *my* obligations, under the constitution, in regard to your slaves. I confess I hate to see the poor creatures hunted down, and caught, and carried back to their stripes, and unrewarded toils; but I bite my lip and keep quiet. In 1841 you and I had together a tedious low-water trip, on a Steam Boat from Louisville to St. Louis. You may remember, as I well do, that from Louisville to the mouth of the Ohio there were, on board, ten or a dozen slaves, shackled together with irons. That sight was a continual torment to me; and I see something like it every time I touch the Ohio, or any other slave-border. It is hardly fair for you to assume, that I have no interest in a thing which has, and continually exercises, the power of making me miserable. You ought rather to appreciate how much the great body of the Northern people do crucify their feelings, in order to maintain their loyalty to the constitution and the Union.

☆

FROM A LETTER TO
GEORGE ROBERTSON, 1855

Another Kentuckian, law professor George Robertson, elicited a letter that reads like a rehearsal of the kind of anti-slavery rhetoric Lincoln was beginning to express in public—including, in the final paragraph, an anticipation of the "House Divided" speech that would help to make Lincoln a national figure.

You are not a friend of slavery in the abstract. In that speech you spoke of *"the peaceful extinction of slavery"* and used other expressions indicating your belief that the thing was, at some time, to have an end[.] Since then we have had thirty six years of experience; and this experience has demonstrated, I think, that there is no peaceful extinction of slavery in prospect for us. The signal failure of Henry Clay, and other good and great men, in 1849, to effect any thing in favor of gradual emancipation in Kentucky, together with a thousand other signs, extinguishes that hope utterly. On the question of liberty, as a principle, we are not what we have been. When we were the political slaves of King George, and wanted to be free, we called the maxim that "all men are created equal" a self evident truth; but now when we have grown fat, and have lost all dread of being slaves ourselves, we have become so greedy to be *masters* that we call the same maxim "a self-evident lie" The fourth of July has not quite dwindled away; it is still a great day—*for burning firecrackers* ! ! !

. . . So far as peaceful, voluntary emancipation is concerned, the condition of the negro slave in America, scarcely less terrible to the contemplation of a free mind, is now as fixed, and hopeless of change for the better, as that of the lost souls of the finally impenitent. The Autocrat of all the Russias will resign his crown, and proclaim his subjects free republicans sooner than will our

American masters voluntarily give up their slaves.

Our political problem now is "Can we, as a nation, continue together *permanently—forever*—half slave, and half free?" The problem is too mighty for me. May God, in his mercy, superintend the solution. Your much obliged friend, and humble servant

A. LINCOLN—

☆

FROM THE SPEECH AT PEORIA
October 16, 1854

This is the prototype of the speech that made Lincoln a national figure and, six years later, President of the United States. In the years to come he would repeat, refine and elaborate the speech hundreds of times, from frontier towns to the Cooper Institute in New York City. On every occasion there was a personal target— Senator Stephen Douglas of Lincoln's home state, his old rival in politics and love, who was chief spokesman for the policy of accommodating the slaveholding states by permitting the extension of slavery to the North and the West. There was a political target, the Kansas-Nebraska Act of 1854, which opened the question of slavery to a vote in the Western territories. And there was a philosophical target, the notion that slavery was morally acceptable and consistent with the principles of the nation. In each speech, too, Lincoln would begin by trying to reassure the South that he wasn't advocating sudden abolition or any measures that might drive it out of the Union.

Before proceeding, let me say I think I have no prejudice against the Southern people. They are just what we would be in their situation. If slavery did not now exist amongst them, they would not introduce it. If it did now exist amongst us, we should not instantly give it up. This I believe of the masses north and south. Doubtless there are individuals, on both sides, who would not hold slaves under any circumstances; and others who would gladly introduce slavery anew, if it were out of existence. We know that some southern men do free their slaves, go north, and become tip-top abolitionists; while some northern ones go south, and become most cruel slave-masters.

When southern people tell us they are no more responsible for the origin of slavery, than we; I acknowledge the fact. When it is said that the institution exists; and that it is very difficult to get rid of it, in any satisfactory way, I can understand and appreciate the saying. I surely will not blame them for not doing what I should not know how to do myself. If all earthly power were given me, I should not know what to do, as to the existing institution. . . .

I trust I understand, and truly estimate the right of self-government. My faith in the proposition that each man should do precisely as he pleases with all which is exclusively his own, lies at the foundation of the sense of justice there is in me. I extend the principles to communities of men, as well as to individuals. I so extend it, because it is politically wise, as well as naturally just: politically wise, in saving us from broils about matters which do not concern us. Here, or at Washington, I would not trouble myself with the oyster laws of Virginia, or the cranberry laws of Indiana.

The doctrine of self government is right—absolutely and eternally right—but it has no just application, as here attempted. Or perhaps I should rather say that whether it has such just application depends upon whether a negro is *not* or *is* a man. If he is *not* a man, why in that case, he who *is* a man may, as a matter of self-government, do just as he pleases with him. But if the negro *is* a man, is it not to that extent, a total destruction of self-government, to say that he too shall not govern *himself?* When the white man governs himself that is self-government; but when he governs himself, and also governs *another* man, that is *more* than self-government—that is despotism. If the negro is a *man*, why then my ancient faith teaches me that "all men are created equal;" and that there can be no moral right in connection with one man's making a slave of another.

Judge Douglas frequently, with bitter irony and sarcasm, paraphrases our argument by saying "The white people of Nebraska are good enough to govern themselves, *but they are not good enough to govern a few miserable negroes!!*"

Well I doubt not that the people of Nebraska are, and will continue to be as good as the average of people elsewhere. I do not say the contrary. What I do say is, that no man is good enough to govern another man, *without that other's consent*. I say this is the leading principle—the sheet anchor of American republicanism. . . .

☆

ACCEPTANCE SPEECH AT THE ILLINOIS STATE CONVENTION, 1858: THE "HOUSE DIVIDED" PASSAGE

Lincoln continued to voice the conservative opposition to slavery— do nothing to interfere with slavery in the South, but nothing to encourage its extension or perpetuation—and in 1856 he made more than 50 speeches on behalf of the Republican Party's first presidential candidate, John C. Frémont. In 1858, Lincoln was the new party's unanimous choice to run against Stephen Douglas for the U.S. Senate. The opening of his acceptance speech got the campaign off to an explosive start.

Mr. PRESIDENT and Gentlemen of the Convention.

If we could first know *where* we are, and *whither* we are tending, we could then better judge *what* to do, and *how* to do it.

We are now far into the *fifth* year, since a policy was initiated, with the *avowed* object, and *confident* promise, of putting an end to slavery agitation.

Under the operation of that policy, that agitation has not only, *not ceased*, but has *constantly augmented*.

In *my* opinion, it *will* not cease, until a *crisis* shall have been reached, and passed.

"A house divided against itself cannot stand."

I believe this government cannot endure, permanently half *slave* and half *free*.

I do not expect the Union to be *dissolved*—I do not expect the house to *fall*—but I *do* expect it will cease to be divided.

It will become *all* one thing, or *all* the other.

Either the *opponents* of slavery, will arrest the further spread of it, and place it where the public mind shall rest in the belief that it is in course of ultimate extinction; or its *advocates* will push it forward, till it shall become alike lawful in *all* the States, *old* as well as *new*—*North* as well as *South*.

Have we no *tendency* to the latter condition?

☆

FROM THE FIRST DEBATE WITH DOUGLAS AT OTTAWA, ILLINOIS

August 21, 1858

Lincoln's lively campaign against Douglas reached its peak in the seven encounters in which they shared a platform and answered each other directly. Lincoln's chances of winning the election were slight, and he knew it. But he campaigned as if he understood that a larger prize than the Illinois Senate seat might be at stake. In the first debate, at Ottawa, Douglas opened and Lincoln followed in reply.

MY FELLOW-CITIZENS: When a man hears himself somewhat misrepresented, it provokes him—at least, I find it so with myself; but when the misrepresentation becomes very gross and palpable, it is more apt to amuse him. [Laughter.]. . . .

Now gentlemen, I hate to waste my time on such things, but in regard to that general abolition tilt that Judge Douglas makes, when he says that I was engaged at that time in selling out and abolitionizing the old Whig party—I hope you will permit me to read a part of a printed speech that I made then at Peoria, which will show altogether a different view of the position I took in that contest of 1854.

VOICE—Put on your specs.

MR. LINCOLN—Yes, sir, I am obliged to do so. I am no longer a young man. [Laughter.]. . . .

Now gentlemen, I don't want to read at any greater length, but this is the true complexion of all I have ever said in regard to the institution of slavery and the black race. This is the whole of it, and anything that argues me into his idea of perfect social and political equality with the negro, is but a specious and fantastic arrangement of words, by which a man can prove a horse chestnut to be a chestnut horse. [Laughter.] I will say here, while upon this subject, that I have no purpose directly or indirectly to interfere with the institution of slavery in the States where it exists. I believe I have no lawful right to do so, and I have no inclination to do so. . . .

Now I pass on to consider one or two more of these little follies. The Judge is wofully at fault about his early friend Lincoln being a "grocery* keeper." [Laughter.] I don't know as it would be a great sin, if I had been, but he is mistaken. Lincoln never kept a grocery anywhere in the world. [Laughter.] It is

* Grocery: i.e., a tavern or liquor store—L. S.

true that Lincoln did work the latter part of one winter in a small still house, up at the head of a hollow. [Roars of laughter.] And so I think my friend, the Judge, is equally at fault when he charges me at the time when I was in Congress of having opposed our soldiers who were fighting in the Mexican war. The Judge did not make his charge very distinctly but I can tell you what he can prove by referring to the record. You remember I was an old Whig, and whenever the Democratic party tried to get me to vote that the war had been righteously begun by the President, I would not do it. But whenever they asked for any money, or land warrants, or anything to pay the soldiers there, during all that time, I gave the same votes that Judge Douglas did. [Loud applause.] You can think as you please as to whether that was consistent. Such is the truth; and the Judge has the right to make all he can out of it. But when he, by a general charge, conveys the idea that I withheld supplies from the soldiers who were fighting in the Mexican war, or did anything else to hinder the soldiers, he is, to say the least, grossly and altogether mistaken, as a consultation of the records will prove to him.

As I have not used up so much of my time as I had supposed, I will dwell a little longer upon one or two of these minor topics upon with the Judge has spoken. He has read from my speech in Springfield, in which I say that "a house divided against itself cannot stand." Does the Judge say it *can* stand? [Laughter.] I don't know whether he does or not. The Judge does not seem to be attending to me just now, but I would like to know if it is his opinion that a house divided against itself *can stand*. If he does, then there is a question of veracity, not between him and me, but between the Judge and an authority of a somewhat higher character. [Laughter and applause.] . . .

. . . Henry Clay, my beau ideal of a statesman, the man for whom I fought all my humble life—Henry Clay once said of a class of men who would repress all tendencies to liberty and ultimate emancipation, that they must, if they would do this, go back to the era of our Independence, and muzzle the cannon which thunders its annual joyous return; they must blow out the moral lights around us; they must penetrate the human soul, and eradicate there the love of liberty; and then and not till then, could they perpetuate slavery in this country! [Loud cheers.] To my thinking, Judge Douglas is, by his example and vast influence, doing that very thing in this community, [cheers,] when he says that the negro has nothing in the Declaration of Independence. Henry Clay plainly understood the contrary. Judge Douglas is going back to the era of our Revolution, and to the extent of his ability, muzzling the cannon which thunders its annual joyous return. When he invites any people willing to have slavery, to establish it, he is blowing out the moral lights around us. [Cheers.] When he says he "cares not whether slavery is voted down or voted up,"—that it is a sacred right of self government—he is in my judgment penetrating the human soul and eradicating the light of reason and the love of liberty in this American people. [Enthusiastic and continued applause.]

☆

FROM THE COOPER UNION ADDRESS
February 27, 1860

After losing to Douglas, Lincoln continued to speak out against the extension of slavery, and in early 1860, the presidential election year, he made a crucial speaking tour of the East Coast. His most important stop was at the Cooper Union in New York City, where his audience was probably the most influential he had ever addressed. Lincoln's speech was an impassioned advocacy of the middle ground: do nothing to encourage slavery, but nothing to interfere with the institution where it already existed.

If slavery is right, all words, acts, laws, and constitutions against it, are themselves wrong, and should be silenced, and swept away. If it is right, we cannot justly object to its nationality —its universality; if it is wrong, they cannot justly insist upon its extension—its enlargment. All they ask, we could readily grant, if we thought slavery right; all we ask, they could as readily grant, if they thought it wrong. Their thinking it right, and our thinking it wrong, is the precise fact upon which depends the whole controversy. Thinking it right, as they do, they are not to blame for desiring its full recognition, as being right; but, thinking it wrong, as we do, can we yield to them? Can we cast our votes with their view, and against our own? In view of our moral, social, and political responsibilities, can we do this?

Wrong as we think slavery is, we can yet afford to let it alone where it is, because that much is due to the necessity arising from its actual presence in the nation; but can we, while our votes will prevent it, allow it to spread into the National Territories, and to overrun us here in these Free States? If our sense of duty forbids this, then let us stand by our duty, fearlessly and effectively. Let us be diverted by none of those sophistical contrivances wherewith we are so industriously plied and belabored —contrivances such as groping for some middle ground between the right and the wrong, vain as the search for a man who should be neither a living man nor a dead man—such as a policy of "don't care" on a question about which all true men do care— such as Union appeals beseeching true Union men to yield to Disunionists, reversing the divine rule, and calling, not the sinners, but the righteous to repentance—such as invocations to Washington, imploring men to unsay what Washington said, and undo what Washington did.

Neither let us be slandered from our duty by false accusations against us, nor frightened from it by menaces of destruction to the Government nor of dungeons to ourselves. LET US HAVE

FAITH THAT RIGHT MAKES MIGHT, AND IN THAT FAITH, LET US,
TO THE END, DARE TO DO OUR DUTY AS WE UNDERSTAND IT.

☆

LETTER TO MARY TODD LINCOLN,
1860

A note from the speaking tour that would help Lincoln win the Republican nomination at the convention in June.

[Exeter, N.H. March 4, 1860]

I have been unable to escape this toil. If I had foreseen it, I
think I would not have come east at all. The speech at New
York, being within my calculation before I started, went off
passably well and gave me no trouble whatever. The difficulty
was to make nine others, before reading audiences who had
already seen all my ideas in print.

☆

☆ III ☆

"Essentially a People's Contest"

FAREWELL ADDRESS,
SPRINGFIELD, 1861

Lincoln delivered these remarks from the rear platform of a train that would take him to Washington, D.C. Now President-elect, he had been out of office more than ten years and had never held an executive position. But there's little sense of triumph in his farewell.

February 11, 1861

My friends—No one, not in my situation, can appreciate my feeling of sadness at this parting. To this place, and the kindness of these people, I owe every thing. Here I have lived a quarter of a century, and have passed from a young to an old man. Here my children have been born, and one is buried. I now leave, not knowing when, or whether ever, I may return, with a task before me greater than that which rested upon Washington. Without the assistance of that Divine Being, who ever attended him, I cannot succeed. With that assistance I cannot fail. Trusting in Him, who can go with me, and remain with you and be every where for good, let us confidently hope that all will yet be well. To His care commending you, as I hope in your prayers you will commend me, I bid you an affectionate farewell

☆

SPEECH AT INDEPENDENCE HALL,
PHILADELPHIA, 1861

In the period between his election and his inauguration Lincoln avoided saying anything that might provoke the South into rebellion, and on his journey from Springfield to Washington he tried to say nothing at all about the nation's crisis. But when he stopped in

*Philadelphia, he learned that there was a plot to assassinate him
in Baltimore, and at Independence Hall he was stirred by the presence of a symbol he held sacred.*

February 22, 1861

Mr. CUYLER:—I am filled with deep emotion at finding myself standing here in the place where were collected together the
wisdom, the patriotism, the devotion to principle, from which
sprang the institutions under which we live. You have kindly
suggested to me that in my hands is the task of restoring peace to
our distracted country. I can say in return, sir, that all the political sentiments I entertain have been drawn, so far as I have been
able to draw them, from the sentiments which originated, and
were given to the world from this hall in which we stand. I have
never had a feeling politically that did not spring from the sentiments embodied in the Declaration of Independence. (Great
cheering.) I have often pondered over the dangers which were
incurred by the men who assembled here and adopted that
Declaration of Independence— I have pondered over the toils
that were endured by the officers and soldiers of the army, who
achieved that Independence. (Applause.) I have often inquired
of myself, what great principle or idea it was that kept this Confederacy so long together. It was not the mere matter of the
separation of the colonies from the mother land; but something
in that Declaration giving liberty, not alone to the people of this
country, but hope to the world for all future time. (Great applause.) It was that which gave promise that in due time the
weights should be lifted from the shoulders of all men, and that
all should have an equal chance. (Cheers.) This is the sentiment
embodied in that Declaration of Independence.

Now, my friends, can this country be saved upon that basis? If
it can, I will consider myself one of the happiest men in the world
if I can help to save it. If it can't be saved upon that principle, it

will be truly awful. But, if this country cannot be saved without giving up that principle—I was about to say I would rather be assassinated on this spot than to surrender it. (Applause.)

Now, in my view of the present aspect of affairs, there is no need of bloodshed and war. There is no necessity for it. I am not in favor of such a course, and I may say in advance, there will be no blood shed unless it be forced upon the Government. The Government will not use force unless force is used against it. (Prolonged applause and cries of "That's the proper sentiment.")

My friends, this is a wholly unprepared speech. I did not expect to be called upon to say a word when I came here—I supposed I was merely to do something towards raising a flag. I may, therefore, have said something indiscreet, (cries of "no, no"), but I have said nothing but what I am willing to live by, and, in the pleasure of Almighty God, die by.

☆

FROM THE
FIRST INAUGURAL ADDRESS, 1861

Could a speech save the Union? Lincoln began work on his First Inaugural before leaving Springfield, and in Washington he consulted with Douglas and Seward in an attempt to assemble as many compelling reasons as possible why the South should not secede. He labored over the address as if he believed that the right combination of arguments and images could yet heal the nation's wounds.

March 4, 1861

Fellow citizens of the United States:

In compliance with a custom as old as the government itself, I appear before you to address you briefly, and to take, in your presence, the oath prescribed by the Constitution of the United

States, to be taken by the President "before he enters on the execution of his office."

I do not consider it necessary, at present, for me to discuss those matters of administration about which there is no special anxiety, or excitement.

Apprehension seems to exist among the people of the Southern States, that by the accession of a Republican Administration, their property, and their peace, and personal security, are to be endangered. There has never been any reasonable cause for such apprehension. Indeed, the most ample evidence to the contrary has all the while existed, and been open to their inspection. It is found in nearly all the published speeches of him who now addresses you. . . .

Physically speaking, we cannot separate. We cannot remove our respective sections from each other, nor build an impassable wall between them. A husband and wife may be divorced, and go out of the presence, and beyond the reach of each other; but the different parts of our country cannot do this. They cannot but remain face to face; and intercourse, either amicable or hostile, must continue between them. Is it possible then to make that intercourse more advantageous, or more satisfactory, *after* separation than *before?* Can aliens make treaties easier than friends can make laws? Can treaties be more faithfully enforced between aliens, than laws can among friends? Suppose you go to war, you cannot fight always; and when, after much loss on both sides, and no gain on either, you cease fighting, the identical old questions, as to terms of intercourse, are again upon you.

This country, with its institutions, belongs to the people who inhabit it. Whenever they shall grow weary of the existing government, they can exercise their *constitutional* right of amending it, or their *revolutionary* right to dismember, or overthrow it. I can not be ignorant of the fact that many worthy, and patriotic citizens are desirous of having the national constitution amended. While I make no recommendation of amendments, I fully recognize the rightful authority of the people over the whole subject, to be exercised in either of the modes prescribed in the instrument itself; and I should, under existing circumstances, favor, rather than oppose, a fair opportunity being afforded the people to act upon it. . . .

My countrymen, one and all, think calmly and *well*, upon this whole subject. Nothing valuable can be lost by taking time. If there be an object to *hurry* any of you, in hot haste, to a step which you would never take *deliberately*, that object will be frustrated by taking time; but no good object can be frustrated by it. Such of you as are now dissatisfied, still have the old Constitution unimpaired, and, on the sensitive point, the laws of your own framing under it; while the new administration will have no immediate power, if it would, to change either. If it were admitted that you who are dissatisfied, hold the right side in the dispute, there still is no single good reason for precipitate action. Intelligence, patriotism, Christianity, and a firm reliance on Him, who has never yet forsaken this favored land, are still competent to adjust, in the best way, all our present difficulty.

In *your* hands, my dissatisfied fellow countrymen, and not in *mine*, is the momentous issue of civil war. The government will not assail *you*. You can have no conflict, without being yourselves the aggressors. *You* have no oath registered in Heaven to destroy the government, while *I* shall have the most solemn one to "preserve, protect and defend" it.

I am loth to close. We are not enemies, but friends. We must not be enemies. Though passion may have strained, it must not break our bonds of affection. The mystic chords of memory, stretching from every battle-field, and patriot grave, to every living heart and hearthstone, all over this broad land, will yet swell the chorus of the Union, when again touched, as surely they will be, by the better angels of our nature.

☆

FROM THE MESSAGE TO CONGRESS
IN SPECIAL SESSION
July 1861

When the war came, Lincoln took care to define it as a war of democracy against despotism, "a people's contest," instead of a war against slavery. As a practical matter, the President wanted to retain the loyalty of slaveholding border states that hadn't seceded, and he wanted to make it as easy as possible for rebellious states to end their rebellion. But at this point Lincoln also still held to his conviction that slavery should not be abolished abruptly because of the economic consequences and what he imagined would be insoluble social problems.

And the issue embraces more than the fate of these United States. It presents to the whole family of man, the question, whether a constitutional republic, or a democracy—a government of the people, by the same people—can, or cannot, maintain its territorial integrity, against its own domestic foes. It presents the question, whether discontented individuals, too few in numbers to control administration, according to organic law, in any case, can always, upon the pretences made in this case, or on any other pretences, or arbitrarily, without any pretence, break up their Government, and thus practically put an end to free government upon the earth. It forces us to ask: "Is there, in all republics, this inherent, and fatal weakness?" "Must a government, of necessity, be too *strong* for the liberties of its own people, or too *weak* to maintain its own existence?" . . .

•   •   •

This is essentially a People's contest. On the side of the Union, it is a struggle for maintaining in the world, that form, and substance of government, whose leading object is, to elevate the condition of men—to lift artificial weights from all shoulders—to clear the paths of laudable pursuit for all—to afford all, an unfettered start, and a fair chance, in the race of life. Yielding to partial, and temporary departures, from necessity, this is the leading object of the government for whose existence we contend.

I am most happy to believe that the plain people understand, and appreciate this. It is worthy of note, that while in this, the government's hour of trial, large numbers of those in the Army and Navy, who have been favored with the offices, have resigned, and proved false to the hand which had pampered them, not one common soldier, or common sailor is known to have deserted his flag.

☆

LETTER TO COLONEL ELLSWORTH'S PARENTS, 1861

Throughout the war, Lincoln's letters of condolence helped to establish his image as a compassionate leader and to offset newspaper portrayals of him as a bungler who didn't care how many lives he sacrificed. Colonel Elmer Ellsworth, the first commissioned officer to be killed in the war, was shot by a hotel keeper in Alexandria, Virginia, while trying to remove a Confederate flag from the roof of the hotel. He had been a clerk in Lincoln's law office in Springfield and had accompanied Lincoln on the train to Washington.

To the Father and Mother of Col.   Washington D.C.
Elmer E. Ellsworth: May 25. 1861

My dear Sir and Madam, In the untimely loss of your noble son, our affliction here, is scarcely less than your own. So much of promised usefulness to one's country, and of bright hopes for one's self and friends, have rarely been so suddenly dashed, as in his fall. In size, in years, and in youthful appearance, a boy only, his power to command men, was surpassingly great. This power, combined with a fine intellect, an indomitable energy, and a taste altogether military, constituted in him, as seemed to me, the best natural talent, in that department, I ever knew. And yet he was singularly modest and deferential in social intercourse. My acquaintance with him began less than two years ago; yet through the latter half of the intervening period, it was as intimate as the disparity of our ages, and my engrossing engagements, would permit. To me, he appeared to have no indulgences or pastimes; and I never heard him utter a profane, or an intemperate word. What was conclusive of his good heart, he never forgot his parents. The honors he labored for so laudably, and, in the sad end, so gallantly gave his life, he meant for them, no less than for himself.

In the hope that it may be no intrusion upon the sacredness of your sorrow, I have ventured to address you this tribute to the memory of my young friend, and your brave and early fallen child.

May God give you that consolation which is beyond all earthly power. Sincerely your friend in a common affliction—

A. LINCOLN

☆

LETTER TO
COUNT A. DE GASPARIN, 1862

The Union and the Confederacy were also engaged in a diplomatic war for the support of European governments. One major European supporter of the Union cause, Count de Gasparin, had expressed wonder that the North didn't make better use of its

numerical superiority. Lincoln's answer explains the strategic prob-
lems, but also reminds the Count that as a democratic government
the Union faced special difficulties in mobilizing resources.

Executive Mansion   Washington August 4. 1862

Dear Sir: Your very acceptable letter dated Orbe Canton de Vaud, Switzerland 18th of July 1862 is received. The moral effect was the worst of the affair before Richmond; and that has run its course downward; we are now at a stand, and shall soon be rising again, as we hope. I believe it is true that in men and material, the enemy suffered more than we, in that series of conflicts; while it is certain he is less able to bear it.

With us every soldier is a man of character and must be treated with more consideration than is customary in Europe. Hence our great army for slighter causes than could have prevailed there has dwindled rapidly, bringing the necessity for a new call, earlier than was anticipated. We shall easily obtain the new levy, however. Be not alarmed if you shall learn that we shall have resorted to a draft for part of this. It seems strange, even to me, but it is true, that the Government is now pressed to this course by a popular demand. Thousands who wish not to personally enter the service are nevertheless anxious to pay and send substitutes, provided they can have assurance that unwilling persons similarly situated will be compelled to do like wise. Besides this, volunteers mostly choose to enter newly forming regiments, while drafted men can be sent to fill up the old ones, wherein, man for man, they are quite doubly as valuable.

You ask "why is it that the North with her great armies, so often is found, with inferiority of numbers, face to face with the armies of the South?" While I painfully know the fact, a military man, which I am not, would better answer the question. The fact I know, has not been overlooked; and I suppose the cause of its continuance lies mainly in the other facts that the enemy holds the interior, and we the exterior lines; and that we operate where the people convey information to the enemy, while he operates where they convey none to us.

I have received the volume and letter which you did me the honor of addressing to me, and for which please accept my sincere thanks. You are much admired in America for the ability of your writings, and much loved for your generosity to us, and your devotion to liberal principles generally.

You are quite right, as to the importance to us, for its bearing upon Europe, that we should achieve military successes; and the same is true for us at home as well as abroad. Yet it seems unreasonable that a series of successes, extending through half-a-year, and clearing more than a hundred thousand square miles of country, should help us so little, while a single half-defeat should hurt us so much. But let us be patient.

I am very happy to know that my course has not conflicted with your judgement, of propriety and policy.

I can only say that I have acted upon my best convictions without selfishness or malice, and that by the help of God, I shall continue to do so.

Please be assured of my highest respect and esteem.

☆

LETTER TO HORACE GREELEY, 1862

Not every Northerner was satisfied with Lincoln's vision of the war as "a people's contest." Greeley, editor of the New York Tribune, *had attacked Lincoln in his paper for not fighting the war to abolish slavery. Although Lincoln had already prepared a statement on emancipation and was awaiting an occasion to issue it, such as a major Union victory, he answered Greeley by insisting that there was a larger issue than slavery at stake in the war.*

Hon. Horace Greely: Executive Mansion,
Dear Sir   Washington, August 22, 1862.

I have just read yours of the 19th. addressed to myself through the New-York Tribune. . . .

As to the policy I "seem to be pursuing" as you say, I have not meant to leave any one in doubt.

I would save the Union. I would save it the shortest way under the Constitution. The sooner the national authority can be restored; the nearer the Union will be "the Union as it was." If there be those who would not save the Union, unless they could at the same time *save* slavery, I do not agree with them. If there be those who would not save the Union unless they could at the same time *destroy* slavery, I do not agree with them. My paramount object in this struggle *is* to save the Union, and is *not* either to save or to destroy slavery. If I could save the Union without freeing *any* slave I would do it, and if I could save it by freeing *all* the slaves I would do it; and if I could save it by freeing some and leaving others alone I would also do that. What I do about slavery, and the colored race, I do because I believe it helps to save the Union; and what I forbear, I forbear because I do *not* believe it would help to save the Union. I shall do *less* whenever I shall believe what I am doing hurts the cause, and I shall do *more* whenever I shall believe doing more will help the cause. I shall try to correct errors when shown to be errors; and I shall adopt new views so fast as they shall appear to be true views.

I have here stated my purpose according to my view of *official* duty; and I intend no modification of my oft-expressed *personal* wish that all men every where could be free. Yours,

A. LINCOLN

☆

☆ IV ☆
Lincoln to His Generals
"*Maxims of War*"

LETTER TO GENERAL
DON CARLOS BUELL, 1862

Lincoln, whose experience in the military was limited to three months in a militia troop during a brief Indian war, when the only enemy he saw wandered into camp by mistake, had to think about strategy and tactics for the first time when he became commander-in-chief. Because he was dealing with sensitive egos and even with a potential rival in George McClellan, he also had to become a psychologist of the military mind. This letter to General Buell, commander of the theater that included most of Kentucky, contains some basic theorizing by the novice military strategist.

C O P Y — one also sent to Gen. Halleck.

Brig. Genl. Buell.   Executive Mansion,
My dear Sir: Washington, Jan. 13, 1862.

Your despatch of yesterday is received, in which you say "I have received your letter and Gen. McClellan's; and will, at once devote all my efforts to your views, and his." In the midst of my many cares, I have not seen, or asked to see, Gen. McClellan's letter to you. For my own views, I have not offered, and do not now offer them as orders; and while I am glad to have them respectfully considered, I would blame you to follow them contrary to your own clear judgment—unless I should put them in the form of orders. As to Gen. McClellan's views, you understand your duty in regard to them better than I do. With this preliminary, I state my general idea of this war to be that we have the *greater* numbers, and the enemy has the *greater* facility of concentrating forces upon points of collision; that we must fail, unless we can find some way of making *our* advantage an over-match for *his*; and that this can only be done by menacing him with superior forces at *different* points, at the *same* time; so that we can safely attack, one, or both, if he makes no change; and if he *weakens* one to *strengthen* the other, forbear to attack the strengthened one, but seize, and hold the weakened one, gaining so much. To illustrate, suppose last summer, when Winchester ran away to re-inforce Mannassas, we had forborne to attack Mannassas, but had seized and held Winchester. I mention this to illustrate, and not to criticise. I did not lose confidence in McDowell, and I think less harshly of Patterson than some others seem to. In application of the general rule I am suggesting, every particular case will have its modifying circumstances, among which the most constantly present, and most difficult to meet, will be the want of perfect knowledge of the enemies' movements. This had it's part in the Bull-Run case; but worse, in that case, was the expiration of the terms of the three months men. Applying the principle to your case, my idea is that Halleck shall menace Columbus, and "down river" generally; while you menace Bowling-Green, and East Tennessee. If the enemy shall concentrate at Bowling-Green, do not retire from his front; yet do not fight him there, either, but seize Columbus and East Tennessee, one or both, left exposed by the concentration at Bowling Green. It is matter of no small anxiety to me and one which I am sure you will not over-look, that the East Tennessee line, is so long, and over so bad a road. Yours very truly

A. LINCOLN

☆

LETTER TO
GENERAL GEORGE McCLELLAN, 1862

At issue was the campaign against Richmond. Lincoln favored a direct advance south from Washington, while McClellan devised a more complicated attack by land and water. The President allowed the general to have his way.

Executive Mansion,

Major General McClellan   Washington, Feb. 3, 1862.

My dear Sir: You and I have distinct, and different plans for a movement of the Army of the Potomac—yours to be down the Chesapeake, up the Rappahannock to Urbana, and across land to the terminus of the Railroad on the York River—, mine to move directly to a point on the Railroad South West of Manassas.

If you will give me satisfactory answers to the following questions, I shall gladly yield my plan to yours.

1st. Does not your plan involve a greatly larger expenditure of *time*, and *money* than mine?

2nd. Wherein is a victory *more certain* by your plan than mine?

3rd. Wherein is a victory *more valuable* by your plan than mine?

4th. In fact, would it not be *less* valuable, in this, that it would break no great line of the enemie's communications, while mine would?

5th. In case of disaster, would not a safe retreat be more difficult by your plan than by mine? Yours truly   A. LINCOLN

☆

LETTER TO GENERAL McCLELLAN, 1862

McClellan's plans for the Peninsular campaign led to another disagreement with Lincoln over whether the general was leaving enough troops to defend Washington and whether the President was allowing enough troops for the general to carry out his plan.

Major General McClellan.   Washington,

My dear Sir.   April 9. 1862

Your despatches complaining that you are not properly sustained, while they do not offend me, do pain me very much.

Blencker's Division was withdrawn from you before you left

here; and you knew the pressure under which I did it, and, as I thought, acquiesced in it—certainly not without reluctance.

After you left, I ascertained that less than twenty thousand unorganized men, without a single field battery, were all you designed to be left for the defence of Washington, and Manassas Junction; and part of this even, was to go to Gen. Hooker's old position. Gen. Banks' corps, once designed for Manassas Junction, was diverted, and tied up on the line of Winchester and Strausburg, and could not leave it without again exposing the upper Potomac, and the Baltimore and Ohio Railroad. This presented, (or would present, when McDowell and Sumner should be gone) a great temptation to the enemy to turn back from the Rappahanock, and sack Washington. My explicit order that Washington should, by the judgment of *all* the commanders of Army corps, be left entirely secure, had been neglected. It was precisely this that drove me to detain McDowell.

I do not forget that I was satisfied with your arrangement to leave Banks at Mannassas Junction; but when that arrangement was broken up, and *nothing* was substituted for it, of course I was not satisfied. I was constrained to substitute something for it myself. And now allow me to ask "Do you really think I should permit the line from Richmond, *via* Mannassas Junction, to this city to be entirely open, except what resistance could be presented by less than twenty thousand unorganized troops?" This is a question which the country will not allow me to evade.

There is a curious mystery about the *number* of the troops now with you. When I telegraphed you on the 6th. saying you had over a hundred thousand with you, I had just obtained from the Secretary of War, a statement, taken as he said, from your own returns, making 108,000 then with you, and *en route* to you. You now say you will have but 85,000, when all *en route* to you shall have reached you. How can the discrepancy of 23,000 be accounted for?

As to Gen. Wool's command, I understand it is doing for you precisely what a like number of your own would have to do, if that command was away.

I suppose the whole force which has gone forward for you, is with you by this time; and if so, I think it is the precise time for you to strike a blow. By delay the enemy will relatively gain upon you—that is, he will gain faster, by *fortifications* and *re-inforcements*, than you can by re-inforcements alone.

And, once more let me tell you, it is indispensable to *you* that you strike a blow. *I* am powerless to help this. You will do me the justice to remember I always insisted, that going down the Bay in search of a field, instead of fighting at or near Mannassas, was only shifting, and not surmounting, a difficulty—that we would find the same enemy, and the same, or equal, intrench-ments, at either place. The country will not fail to note—is now noting—that the present hesitation to move upon an intrenched enemy, is but the story of Manassas repeated.

I beg to assure you that I have never written you, or spoken to you, in greater kindness of feeling than now, nor with a fuller purpose to sustain you, so far as in my most anxious judgment, I consistently can. *But you must act.* Yours very truly

A. LINCOLN

☆

LETTER TO
GENERAL McCLELLAN, 1862

Within a few miles of Richmond, McClellan was attacked and driven southward. In turning down the general's request for 50,000 more troops, Lincoln was careful not to blame him for failure, al-though within a few days he would replace McClellan with Henry W. Halleck as chief of all the Federal armies.

Washington, D.C.,
Major Gen. McClellan   July 2 1862.

Your despatch of Tuesday morning induces me to hope your Army is having some rest. In this hope, allow me to reason with you a moment. When you ask for fifty thousand men to be promptly sent you, you surely labor under some gross mistake of fact. Recently you sent papers showing your disposal of forces, made last spring, for the defence of Washington, and advising a return to that plan. I find it included in, and about Washington seventyfive thousand men. Now please be assured, I have not men enough to fill that very plan by fifteen thousand. All of Fremont in the valley, all of Banks, all of McDowell, not with you, and all in Washington, taken together do not exceed, if they reach sixty thousand. With Wool and Dix added to those mentioned, I have not, outside of your Army, seventyfive thousand men East of the mountains. Thus, the idea of sending you fifty thousand, or any other considerable force promptly, is simply absurd. If in your frequent mention of responsibility, you have the impression that I blame you for not doing more than you can, please be relieved of such impression. I only beg that in like manner, you will not ask impossibilities of me. If you think you are not strong enough to take Richmond just now, I do not ask you to try just now. Save the Army, material and personal; and I will strengthen it for the offensive again, as fast as I can. The Governors of eighteen states offer me a new levy of three hundred thousand, which I accept.   A. LINCOLN

☆

TWO LETTERS TO
GENERAL McCLELLAN, 1862

The victory at Antietam was a major turning point for the Union Army, but McClellan complained afterward of supply and transportation problems and failed to follow up the victory.

Major General McClellan   Executive Mansion,
My dear Sir   Washington, Oct. 13, 1862.

You remember my speaking to you of what I called your over-cautiousness. Are you not over-cautious when you assume that you can not do what the enemy is constantly doing? Should you not claim to be at least his equal in prowess, and act upon the claim?

As I understand, you telegraph Gen. Halleck that you can not subsist your army at Winchester unless the Railroad from Harper's Ferry to that point be put in working order. But the enemy does now subsist his army at Winchester at a distance nearly twice as great from railroad transportation as you would have to do without the railroad last named. He now wagons from Culpepper C.H. which is just about twice as far as you would have to do from Harper's Ferry. He is certainly not more than half as well provided with wagons as you are. I certainly should be pleased for you to have the advantage of the Railroad from Harper's Ferry to Winchester, but it wastes all the remainder of autumn to give it to you; and, in fact ignores the question of *time*, which can not, and must not be ignored.

Again, one of the standard maxims of war, as you know, is "to operate upon the enemy's communications as much as possible without exposing your own." You seem to act as if this applies *against* you, but can not apply in your *favor*. Change positions with the enemy, and think you not he would break your communication with Richmond within the next twentyfour hours?

☆ 57 ☆

You dread his going into Pennsylvania. But if he does so in full force, he gives up his communications to you absolutely, and you have nothing to do but to follow, and ruin him; if he does so with less than full force, fall upon, and beat what is left behind all the easier. . . .

You know I desired, but did not order, you to cross the Potomac below, instead of above the Shenandoah and Blue Ridge. My idea was that this would at once menace the enemies' communications, which I would seize if he would permit. If he should move Northward I would follow him closely, holding his communications. If he should prevent our seizing his communications, and move towards Richmond, I would press closely to him, fight him if a favorable opportunity should present, and, at least, try to beat him to Richmond on the inside track. I say "try"; if we never try, we shall never succeed. If he make a stand at Winchester, moving neither North or South, I would fight him there, on the idea that if we can not beat him when he bears the wastage of coming to us, we never can when we bear the wastage of going to him. This proposition is a simple truth, and is too important to be lost sight of for a moment. In coming to us, he tenders us an advantage which we should not waive. We should not so operate as to merely drive him away. As we must beat him somewhere, or fail finally, we can do it, if at all, easier near to us, than far away. If we can not beat the enemy where he now is, we never can, he again being within the entrenchments of Richmond. . . .

I should think it preferable to take the route nearest the enemy, disabling him to make an important move without your knowledge, and compelling him to keep his forces together, for dread of you. The gaps would enable you to attack if you should wish. For a great part of the way, you would be practically between the enemy and both Washington and Richmond, enabling us to spare you the greatest number of troops from here. When at length, running for Richmond ahead of him enables him to move this way; if he does so, turn and attack him in rear. But I think he should be engaged long before such point is reached. It is all easy if our troops march as well as the enemy; and it is unmanly to say they can not do it.

This letter is in no sense an order. Yours truly   A. LINCOLN.

Washington City, D.C.

Majr. Genl. McClellan   Oct. 24 [25]. 1862

I have just read your despatch about sore tongued and fateigued horses. Will you pardon me for asking what the horses of your army have done since the battle of Antietam that fatigue anything?   A. LINCOLN

☆

LETTER TO GENERAL HOOKER, 1863

In November 1862, Lincoln replaced McClellan as commander of the Army of the Potomac with Ambrose E. Burnside. After the defeat at Fredericksburg in December, Burnside was replaced by Joseph Hooker, who had a reputation as an intriguer.

Major General Hooker: Executive Mansion,
General.   Washington, January 26, 1863.

I have placed you at the head of the Army of the Potomac. Of course I have done this upon what appear to me to be sufficient reasons. And yet I think it best for you to know that there are some things in regard to which, I am not quite satisfied with you. I believe you to be a brave and a skilful soldier, which, of course, I like. I also believe you do not mix politics with your profession, in which you are right. You have confidence in yourself, which is a valuable, if not an indispensable quality. You are ambitious, which, within reasonable bounds, does good rather than harm. But I think that during Gen. Burnside's command of the Army, you have taken counsel of your ambition, and thwarted him as much as you could, in which you did a great wrong to the country, and to a most meritorious and honorable brother officer. I have heard, in such way as to believe it, of your recently saying that both the Army and the Government needed a Dictator. Of course it was not *for* this, but in spite of it, that I have given you the command. Only those generals who gain successes, can set up dictators. What I now ask of you is military success, and I will risk the dictatorship. The government will support you to the utmost of it's ability, which is neither more nor less than it has done and will do for all commanders. I much fear that the spirit which you have aided to infuse into the Army, of criticising their Commander, and withholding confidence from him, will now turn upon you. I shall assist you as far as I can, to put it down. Neither you, nor Napoleon, if he were alive again, could get any good out of an army, while such a spirit prevails in it.

And now, beware of rashness. Beware of rashness, but with energy, and sleepless vigilance, go forward, and give us victories. Yours very truly   A. LINCOLN

☆

LETTER TO GENERAL GRANT, 1863
Lincoln seems greatly relieved to be addressing a general who is neither neurotic nor incompetent.

Major General Grant   Executive Mansion,
My dear General   Washington, July 13, 1863.

I do not remember that you and I ever met personally. I write this now as a grateful acknowledgment for the almost inestimable service you have done the country. I wish to say a word further. When you first reached the vicinity of Vicksburg, I thought you should do, what you finally did—march the troops across the neck, run the batteries with the transports, and thus go below; and I never had any faith, except a general hope that you knew better than I, that the Yazoo Pass expedition, and the like, could succeed. When you got below, and took Port-Gibson, Grand Gulf, and vicinity, I thought you should go down the river and join Gen. Banks; and when you turned Northward East of the Big Black, I feared it was a mistake. I now wish to make the personal acknowledgment that you were right, and I was wrong.

Yours very truly

A. LINCOLN

☆

LETTER TO GENERAL GRANT, 1864

Another note, free of coaxing or coercive flattery, to the commander who had won Lincoln's complete trust.

Executive Mansion Washington,

Lieutenant General Grant.   April 30, 1864

Not expecting to see you again before the Spring campaign opens, I wish to express, in this way, my entire satisfaction with what you have done up to this time, so far as I understand it. The particulars of your plans I neither know, or seek to know. You are vigilant and self-reliant; and, pleased with this, I wish not to obtrude any constraints or restraints upon you. While I am very anxious that any great disaster, or the capture of our men in great numbers, shall be avoided, I know these points are less likely to escape your attention than they would be mine. If there is anything wanting which is within my power to give, do not fail to let me know it.

And now with a brave Army, and a just cause, may God sustain you. Yours very truly   A. LINCOLN

☆

LETTER TO GENERAL SHERMAN, 1864

Sherman's capture of Atlanta played a part in Lincoln's reelection in November, and now the general offered Savannah to Lincoln as "a Christmas gift."

Executive Mansion, Washington,

My dear General Sherman.   Dec. 26, 1864.

Many, many, thanks for your Christmas-gift—the capture of Savannah.

When you were about leaving Atlanta for the Atlantic coast, I was *anxious*, if not fearful; but feeling that you were the better judge, and remembering that "nothing risked, nothing gained" I did not interfere. Now, the undertaking being a success, the honor is all yours; for I believe none of us went farther than to acquiesce. And, taking the work of Gen. Thomas into the count, as it should be taken, it is indeed a great success. Not only does it afford the obvious and immediate military advantages; but, in showing to the world that your army could be divided, putting the stronger part to an important new service, and yet leaving enough to vanquish the old opposing force of the whole—Hood's army—it brings those who sat in darkness, to see a great light. But what next? I suppose it will be safer if I leave Gen. Grant and yourself to decide.

Please make my grateful acknowledgments to your whole army, officers and men. Yours very truly   A. LINCOLN.

☆

"The Fiery Trial
Through Which
We Pass"

FROM THE ANNUAL MESSAGE
TO CONGRESS

December 1, 1862

In September 1861, McClellan had turned back the Confederate invasion of Maryland at Antietam, and Lincoln seized the opportunity to issue a preliminary emancipation order. Thereafter, as the Confederate military threat receded, Lincoln spoke more of the evils of slavery and of the war as an occasion to root out a historical evil. He spoke less in terms of a political mission and more of a spiritual mission.

The dogmas of the quiet past, are inadequate to the stormy present. The occasion is piled high with difficulty, and we must rise with the occasion. As our case is new, so we must think anew, and act anew. We must disenthrall our selves, and then we shall save our country.

Fellow-citizens, *we* cannot escape history. We of this Congress and this administration, will be remembered in spite of ourselves. No personal significance, or insignificance, can spare one or another of us. The fiery trial through which we pass, will light us down, in honor or dishonor, to the latest generation. We *say* we are for the Union. The world will not forget that we say this. We know how to save the Union. The world knows we do know how to save it. We—even *we here*—hold the power, and bear the responsibility. In *giving* freedom to the *slave*, we *assure* freedom to the *free*—honorable alike in what we give, and what we preserve. We shall nobly save, or meanly lose, the last best, hope of earth. Other means may succeed; this could not fail. The way is plain, peaceful, generous, just—a way which, if followed, the world will forever applaud, and God must forever bless.

ABRAHAM LINCOLN

☆

EMANCIPATION PROCLAMATION, 1863

The Emancipation Proclamation had little immediate practical effect in liberating slaves, but it was of great symbolic import in declaring that emancipation was to be a central goal of the war.

January 1, 1863

By the President of the United States of America:

A Proclamation.

Whereas, on the twentysecond day of September, in the year of our Lord one thousand eight hundred and sixty two, a proclamation was issued by the President of the United States, containing, among other things, the following, towit:

That on the first day of January, in the year of our Lord one thousand eight hundred and sixty-three, all persons held as slaves within any State or designated part of a State, the people whereof shall then be in rebellion against the United States, shall be then, thenceforward, and forever free; and the Executive Government of the United States, including the military and naval authority thereof, will recognize and maintain the freedom of such persons, and will do no act or acts to repress such persons, or any of them, in any efforts they may make for their actual freedom.

That the Executive will, on the first day of January aforesaid, by proclamation, designate the States and parts of States, if any, in which the people thereof, respectively, shall then be in rebellion against the United States; and the fact that any State, or the people thereof, shall on that day be, in good faith, represented in the Congress of the United States by members chosen thereto at elections wherein a majority of the qualified voters of such State shall have participated, shall, in the absence of strong countervailing testimony, be deemed conclusive evidence that such State, and the people thereof, are not then in rebellion against the United States.

Now, therefore I, Abraham Lincoln, President of the United States, by virtue of the power in me vested as Commander-in-Chief, of the Army and Navy of the United States in time of actual armed rebellion against authority and government of the United States, and as a fit and necessary war measure for suppressing said rebellion, do, on this first day of January, in the year of our Lord one thousand eight hundred and sixty three, and in accordance with my purpose so to do publicly proclaimed for the full period of one hundred days, from the day first above mentioned, order and designate as the States and parts of States wherein the people thereof respectively, are this day in rebellion against the United States, the following, towit:

Arkansas, Texas, Louisiana, (except the Parishes of St. Bernard, Plaquemines, Jefferson, St. Johns, St. Charles, St. James[,] Ascension, Assumption, Terrebonne, Lefourche, St. Mary, St. Martin, and Orleans, including the City of New-Orleans) Mississippi, Alabama, Florida, Georgia, South-Carolina, North-Carolina, and Virginia, (except the fortyeight counties designated as West Virginia, and also the counties of Berkley, Accomac, Northampton, Elizabeth-City, York, Princess Ann, and Norfolk, including the cities of Norfolk & Portsmouth [)]; and which excepted parts are, for the present, left precisely as if this proclamation were not issued.

And by virtue of the power, and for the purpose aforesaid, I do order and declare that all persons held as slaves within said designated States, and parts of States, are, and henceforward shall be free; and that the Executive government of the United States, including the military and naval authorities thereof, will recognize and maintain the freedom of said persons.

And I hereby enjoin upon the people so declared to be free to abstain from all violence, unless in necessary self-defence; and I recommend to them that, in all cases when allowed, they labor faithfully for reasonable wages.

And I further declare and make known, that such persons of suitable condition, will be received into the armed service of the United States to garrison forts, positions, stations, and other places, and to man vessels of all sorts in said service.

And upon this act, sincerely believed to be an act of justice, warranted by the Constitution, upon military necessity, I invoke the considerate judgment of mankind, and the gracious favor of Almighty God.

In witness whereof, I have hereunto set my hand and caused the seal of the United States to be affixed.

Done at the City of Washington, this first day of January, in the year of our Lord one thousand eight hundred and sixty three, and of the Independence of the United States of America the eighty-seventh.

By the President: ABRAHAM LINCOLN

WILLIAM H. SEWARD, Secretary of State.

☆

FROM A LETTER
TO JAMES C. CONKLING, 1863

Once Lincoln issued the Emancipation Proclamation, he came under attack from Northerners who said that slavery was not worth a war and that, by adding this issue to the agenda, the President had made it harder to come to terms with the South. This letter, much quoted in the press, helped to establish Lincoln's reputation as the great emancipator.

. . . I know as fully as one can know the opinions of others, that some of the commanders of our armies in the field who have given us our most important successes, believe the emancipation policy, and the use of colored troops, constitute the heaviest blow yet dealt to the rebellion; and that, at least one of those important successes, could not have been achieved when it was, but for the aid of black soldiers. Among the commanders holding these views are some who have never had any affinity with what is called abolitionism, or with republican party politics; but who hold them purely as military opinions. I submit these opinions as being entitled to some weight against the objections, often urged, that emancipation, and arming the blacks, are unwise as military measures, and were not adopted, as such, in good faith.

You say you will not fight to free negroes. Some of them seem willing to fight for you; but, no matter. Fight you, then, exclusively to save the Union. I issued the proclamation on purpose to aid you in saving the Union. Whenever you shall have conquered all resistance to the Union, if I shall urge you to continue fighting, it will be an apt time, then, for you to declare you will not fight to free negroes.

I thought that in your struggle for the Union, to whatever extent the negroes should cease helping the enemy, to that extent it weakened the enemy in his resistance to you. Do you think differently? I thought that whatever negroes can be got to do as soldiers, leaves just so much less for white soldiers to do, in saving the Union. Does it appear otherwise to you? But negroes, like other people, act upon motives. Why should they do any thing for us, if we will do nothing for them? If they stake their lives for us, they must be prompted by the strongest motive— even the promise of freedom. And the promise being made, must be kept. . . .

Peace does not appear so distant as it did. I hope it will come soon, and come to stay; and so come as to be worth the keeping in all future time. It will then have been proved that, among free men, there can be no successful appeal from the ballot to the bullet; and that they who take such appeal are sure to lose their case, and pay the cost. And then, there will be some black men who can remember that, with silent tongue, and clenched teeth, and steady eye, and well-poised bayonet, they have helped mankind on to this great consummation; while, I fear, there will be some white ones, unable to forget that, with malignant heart, and deceitful speech, they have strove to hinder it.

☆

LETTER TO MARY TODD LINCOLN,
1863

Despite the burdens of office and the increasing eccentricity of Mrs. Lincoln, family life for the President continued at its previous level of small vexations and comforts, as this letter testifies.

Executive Mansion, Washington, August 8, 1863. My dear Wife. All as well as usual, and no particular trouble any way. I put the money into the Treasury at five per cent, with the previlege of withdrawing it any time upon thirty days' notice. I suppose you are glad to learn this. Tell dear Tad, poor "Nanny Goat," is lost; and Mrs. Cuthbert & I are in distress about it. The day you left Nanny was found resting herself, and chewing her little cud, on the middle of Tad's bed. But now she's gone! The gardener kept complaining that she destroyed the flowers, till it was concluded to bring her down to the White House. This was done, and the second day she had disappeared, and has not been heard of since. This is the last we know of poor "Nanny"

The weather continues dry, and excessively warm here.

Nothing very important occurring. The election in Kentucky has gone very strongly right. Old Mr. Wickliffe got ugly, as you know, ran for Governor, and is terribly beaten. Upon Mr. Crittendens death, Brutus Clay, Cassius' brother, was put on the track for Congress, and is largely elected. Mr. Menzies, who, as we thought, behaved very badly last session of Congress, is largely beaten in the District opposite Cincinnati, by Green Clay Smith, Cassius Clay's nephew. But enough. Affectionately

A. Lincoln

☆

THE GETTYSBURG ADDRESS
November 19, 1863

Edward Everett, the leading orator of the day, was invited to make the principal address at the ceremonies dedicating the national cemetery. President Lincoln was asked to make a few concluding remarks (it was hoped he wouldn't sully the occasion by telling funny stories). Everett's address lasted two hours, but Lincoln's remarks, which he had prepared with great care, were over almost before the audience had begun to listen—it was said that a man with a camera didn't have time to set up his equipment before Lincoln was finished. Nobody who was there seemed to feel that he had heard a masterpiece of oratory.

Four score and seven years ago our fathers brought forth on this continent, a new nation, conceived in Liberty, and dedicated to the proposition that all men are created equal.

Now we are engaged in a great civil war, testing whether that nation, or any nation so conceived and so dedicated, can long endure. We are met on a great battle-field of that war. We have come to dedicate a portion of that field, as a final resting place for those who here gave their lives that that nation might live. It is altogether fitting and proper that we should do this.

But, in a larger sense, we can not dedicate—we can not consecrate—we can not hallow—this ground. The brave men, living and dead, who struggled here, have consecrated it, far above our poor power to add or detract. The world will little note, nor long remember what we say here, but it can never forget what they did here. It is for us the living, rather, to be dedicated here to the unfinished work which they who fought here have thus far so nobly advanced. It is rather for us to be here dedicated to the great task remaining before us—that from these honored dead we take increased devotion to that cause for which they gave the last full measure of devotion—that we here highly resolve that these dead shall not have died in vain—that this nation, under God, shall have a new birth of freedom—and that government of the people, by the people, for the people, shall not perish from the earth.   ABRAHAM LINCOLN

☆

LETTER TO A. G. HODGES, 1864

This is the source of the famous statement "I claim not to have controlled events, but confess plainly that events have controlled me." The occasion was a protest by Kentuckians, including Hodges, over the use of ex-slaves in the Union Army. Lincoln's reelection campaign was approaching, and it was no time to antagonize the loyal border states, but the army needed the manpower that freed slaves could provide.

A. G. Hodges, Esq   Executive Mansion,
Frankfort, Ky.   Washington, April 4, 1864.

My dear Sir: You ask me to put in writing the substance of what I verbally said the other day, in your presence, to Governor Bramlette and Senator Dixon. It was about as follows:

"I am naturally anti-slavery. If slavery is not wrong, nothing is wrong. I can not remember when I did not so think, and feel. And yet I have never understood that the Presidency conferred upon me an unrestricted right to act officially upon this judg-

ment and feeling. It was in the oath I took that I would, to
the best of my ability, preserve, protect, and defend the Constitution of the United States. I could not take the office without
taking the oath. Nor was it my view that I might take an oath
to get power, and break the oath in using the power. I understood, too, that in ordinary civil administration this oath even
forbade me to practically indulge my primary abstract judgment
on the moral question of slavery. I had publicly declared this
many times, and in many ways. And I aver that, to this day, I
have done no official act in mere deference to my abstract judgment and feeling on slavery. I did understand however, that my
oath to preserve the constitution to the best of my ability, im-
posed upon me the duty of preserving, by every indispensable
means, that government—that nation—of which that constitution was the organic law. Was it possible to lose the nation, and
yet preserve the constitution? By general law life *and* limb must
be protected; yet often a limb must be amputated to save a life;
but a life is never wisely given to save a limb. I felt that measures, otherwise unconstitutional, might become lawful, by be-
coming indispensable to the preservation of the constitution,
through the preservation of the nation. Right or wrong, I assumed this ground, and now avow it. . . . When, in March, and
May, and July 1862 I made earnest, and successive appeals to
the border states to favor compensated emancipation, I believed
the indispensable necessity for military emancipation, and arming the blacks would come, unless averted by that measure. They
declined the proposition; and I was, in my best judgment, driven
to the alternative of either surrendering the Union, and with it,
the Constitution, or of laying strong hand upon the colored ele-
ment. I chose the latter. In choosing it, I hoped for greater gain
than loss; but of this, I was not entirely confident. More than a
year of trial now shows no loss by it in our foreign relations,
none in our home popular sentiment, none in our white military

force,—no loss by it any how or any where. On the contrary, it shows a gain of quite a hundred and thirty thousand soldiers, seamen, and laborers. These are palpable facts, about which, as facts, there can be no cavilling. We have the men; and we could not have had them without the measure.

["]And now let any Union man who complains of the measure, test himself by writing down in one line that he is for subduing the rebellion by force of arms; and in the next, that he is for taking these hundred and thirty thousand men from the Union side, and placing them where they would be but for the measure he condemns. If he can not face his case so stated, it is only because he can not face the truth.["]

I add a word which was not in the verbal conversation. In telling this tale I attempt no compliment to my own sagacity. I claim not to have controlled events, but confess plainly that events have controlled me. Now, at the end of three years struggle the nation's condition is not what either party, or any man devised, or expected. God alone can claim it. Whither it is tending seems plain. If God now wills the removal of a great wrong, and wills also that we of the North as well as you of the South, shall pay fairly for our complicity in that wrong, impartial history will find therein new cause to attest and revere the justice and goodness of God. Yours truly   A. LINCOLN

☆

SPEECH AT A WHITE HOUSE
SERENADE, 1864

These remarks were delivered on the White House lawn to visitors who came to congratulate the President on his reelection victory. It was not, in Lincoln's mind, a fitting occasion for a victory speech.

November 10, 1864

It has long been a grave question whether any government, not *too* strong for the liberties of its people, can be strong *enough* to maintain its own existence, in great emergencies.

On this point the present rebellion brought our republic to a severe test; and a presidential election occurring in regular course during the rebellion added not a little to the strain. If the loyal people, *united*, were put to the utmost of their strength by the rebellion, must they not fail when *divided*, and partially paralized, by a political war among themselves?

But the election was a necessity.

We can not have free government without elections; and if the rebellion could force us to forego, or postpone a national election, it might fairly claim to have already conquered and ruined us. The strife of the election is but human-nature practically applied to the facts of the case. What has occurred in this case, must ever recur in similar cases. Human-nature will not change. In any future great national trial, compared with the men of this, we shall have as weak, and as strong; as silly and as wise; as bad and good. Let us, therefore, study the incidents of this, as philosophy to learn wisdom from, and none of them as wrongs to be revenged.

But the election, along with its incidental, and undesirable strife, has done good too. It has demonstrated that a people's government can sustain a national election, in the midst of a great civil war. Until now it has not been known to the world that this was a possibility. It shows also how *sound*, and how *strong* we still are. It shows that, even among candidates of the same party, he who is most devoted to the Union, and most opposed to treason, can receive most of the people's votes. It shows also, to the extent yet known, that we have more men now, than we had when the war began. Gold is good in its place; but living, brave, patriotic men, are better than gold.

But the rebellion continues; and now that the election is over, may not all, having a common interest, re-unite in a common effort, to save our common country? For my own part I have striven, and shall strive to avoid placing any obstacle in the way. So long as I have been here I have not willingly planted a thorn in any man's bosom.

. . . And now, let me close by asking three hearty cheers for our brave soldiers and seamen and their gallant and skilful commanders.

☆

SECOND INAUGURAL ADDRESS, 1865

The First Inaugural had been built of reasons and argument, like a lawyer's summation to a jury. At the Second Inaugural the time for argument was past, and Lincoln addressed the nation not as its commander-in-chief but as its spiritual leader.

[Fellow Countrymen:]   March 4, 1865

At this second appearing to take the oath of the presidential office, there is less occasion for an extended address than there was at the first. Then a statement, somewhat in detail, of a course to be pursued, seemed fitting and proper. Now, at the expiration of four years, during which public declarations have been constantly called forth on every point and phase of the great contest which still absorbs the attention, and engrosses the enerergies [*sic*] of the nation, little that is new could be presented. The progress of our arms, upon which all else chiefly depends, is as well known to the public as to myself; and it is, I trust, reasonably satisfactory and encouraging to all. With high hope for the future, no prediction in regard to it is ventured.

On the occasion corresponding to this four years ago, all thoughts were anxiously directed to an impending civil-war. All dreaded it—all sought to avert it. While the inaugural address was being delivered from this place, devoted altogether to *saving* the Union without war, insurgent agents were in the city seeking to *destroy* it without war—seeking to dissol[v]e the Union, and divide effects, by negotiation. Both parties deprecated war; but one of them would *make* war rather than let the nation survive; and the other would *accept* war rather than let it perish. And the war came.

One eighth of the whole population were colored slaves, not distributed generally over the Union, but localized in the Southern part of it. These slaves constituted a peculiar and powerful interest. All knew that this interest was, somehow, the cause of the war. To strengthen, perpetuate, and extend this interest was the object for which the insurgents would rend the Union, even by war; while the government claimed no right to do more than to restrict the territorial enlargement of it. Neither party expected for the war, the magnitude, or the duration, which it has already attained. Neither anticipated that the *cause* of the conflict might cease with, or even before, the conflict itself should cease. Each looked for an easier triumph, and a result less fundamental and astounding. Both read the same Bible, and pray to the same God; and each invokes His aid against the other. It may seem strange that any men should dare to ask a just God's assistance in wringing their bread from the sweat of other men's faces; but let us judge not that we be not judged. The prayers of both could not be answered; that of neither has been answered fully. The Almighty has His own purposes. "Woe unto the world because of offences! for it must needs be that offences come; but woe to that man by whom the offence cometh!" If we shall suppose that American Slavery is one of those offences which, in the providence of God, must needs come, but which, having continued through His appointed time, He now wills to remove, and that He gives to both North and South, this terrible war, as the woe due to those by whom the offence came, shall we discern therein any departure from those divine attributes which the believers in a Living God always ascribe to Him? Fondly do we hope—fervently do we pray—that this mighty scourge of war may speedily pass away. Yet, if God wills that it continue, until all the wealth piled by the bond-man's two hundred and fifty years of unrequited toil shall be sunk, and until every drop of blood drawn with the lash, shall be paid by another drawn with the sword, as was said three thousand years ago, so still it must be said "the judgments of the Lord, are true and righteous altogether"

With malice toward none; with charity for all; with firmness in the right, as God gives us to see the right, let us strive on to finish the work we are in; to bind up the nation's wounds; to care for him who shall have borne the battle, and for his widow, and his orphan—to do all which may achieve and cherish a just, and lasting peace, among ourselves, and with all nations.

☆

FROM THE LAST PUBLIC ADDRESS
April 11, 1865

Lincoln's last public remarks were an attempt to explain what he was trying to do to bring the South back into the nation, using Louisiana as an example. It is said that John Wilkes Booth was in the audience and left in a rage over what he heard.

Some twelve thousand voters in the heretofore slave-state of Louisiana have sworn allegiance to the Union, assumed to be the rightful political power of the State, held elections, organized a State government, adopted a free-state constitution, giving the benefit of public schools equally to black and white, and empowering the Legislature to confer the elective franchise upon the colored man. Their Legislature has already voted to ratify the

constitutional amendment recently passed by Congress, abolish-
ing slavery throughout the nation. These twelve thousand persons are thus fully committed to the Union, and to perpetual
freedom in the state—committed to the very things, and nearly
all the things the nation wants—and they ask the nations recognition, and it's assistance to make good their committal. Now, if
we reject, and spurn them, we do our utmost to disorganize and
disperse them. We in effect say to the white men "You are worth-
less, or worse—we will neither help you, nor be helped by you."
To the blacks we say "This cup of liberty which these, your
old masters, hold to your lips, we will dash from you, and leave
you to the chances of gathering the spilled and scattered contents
in some vague and undefined when, where, and how." If this
course, discouraging and paralyzing both white and black, has
any tendency to bring Louisiana into proper practical relations
with the Union, I have, so far, been unable to perceive it. If, on
the contrary, we recognize, and sustain the new government of
Louisiana the converse of all this is made true. We encourage the
hearts, and nerve the arms of the twelve thousand to adhere to
their work, and argue for it, and proselyte for it, and fight for it,
and feed it, and grow it, and ripen it to a complete success. The
colored man too, in seeing all united for him, is inspired with
vigilance, and energy, and daring, to the same end. Grant that he
desires the elective franchise, will he not attain it sooner by saving the already advanced steps toward it, than by running back-
ward over them? Concede that the new government of Louisiana
is only to what it should be as the egg is to the fowl, we shall
sooner have the fowl by hatching the egg than by smashing it?

☆

The text of this book was set on the Linotype in Bodoni Book, a typeface based on the designs of Giambattista Bodoni (1740– 1813). While maintaining the vertical emphasis of the letter with its exaggerated thick and thin strokes, the face is still extremely readable.

The display type, now known as Bell, was originally cut by Richard Austin in 1788 for use in John Bell's newspaper *The Oracle*. This typeface is sharp and crisp yet not as severe as the Bodoni faces, since it was based on more rounded French transitional models. Austin later cut a version of this same letter which became known in this country as Scotch. Both the Scotch and Bodoni faces were widely used during the mid-nineteenth century. Indeed, almost all books printed during the Civil War used some version of them.

Typography by Joe Marc Freedman